264.02

Eucharist
The Body of Christ

D0808335

CONTENTS

1. THE GOSPEL OF LIFE

What is the Gospel basically about? Just sin and forgiveness, or, more fundamentally, life and death? We might often think of it in terms of sin and forgiveness, but Jesus himself points us deeper, to issues of life and death. He summarised the whole purpose of his coming when he simply said: 'I have come so that they may have life and have it to the full' (*Jn* 10:10).[1] The central festival of the Christian year is Easter, when we celebrate Christ's victory, the victory of life over death. St Paul taught that 'the last of the enemies to be done away with is death' (*1 Cor* 15:26), and emphasised that Christ's Resurrection is the ground of our faith and the source of our hope (*1 Cor* 15:12-19). Our Christian lives centre on the fact that he is risen!

The Easter Candle shines the unquenchable light of the risen Jesus into a world which knows the darkness of sin and death, and the core message of the Gospel is that life has overcome death. We go out into the world to proclaim Christ's victory: 'Death has no power over him any more' (*Rom* 6:9). The real cause of our joy is that he shares his victory with us. Easter is the great season for Baptism, and St Paul teaches that in Baptism we die with Christ so as to rise with him. Already, therefore, we share in his victory and in his everlasting life. Paul tells the Romans that 'all of us, when we were baptised into Christ Jesus, were baptised into his death'; 'by our baptism into his death we were buried with him, so that as Christ was raised from the dead by the Father's glorious power, we too should begin living a new life' (*Rom* 6:3-4). This is an immense gift, and we have to learn more about this new life and put it into practice. 'By dying, [Christ] is dead to sin once and for all, and now the life that he lives is life with God. In the same way, you must see yourselves as being dead to sin but alive for God in Christ Jesus.' (*Rom* 6:10-11).

> *By means of the Eucharist, he nurtures and strengthens what he has given us in Baptism*

Learning to see ourselves like this and to live accordingly is a life-long project! It's a journey, on which we will need food and forgiveness, regular contact with the mystery of the death and Resurrection of the Lord, strong companionship, and a vivid awareness of our heavenly destination. To supply all of these, Christ has given us also the sacrament of the Eucharist. By means of the Eucharist, he nurtures and strengthens what he has given us in Baptism. The life which begins in Baptism is sustained, renewed and deepened by the food of life which is the Eucharist: 'this life-giving bread, this saving cup' (Eucharistic Prayer II). The celebration of the

Eucharist is what keeps the mystery of our Baptism fresh until the day we die. At that moment, the dying and rising that was symbolised in Baptism is finally actuated in our lives, our Baptism is consummated, and we close our eyes on this world so as to open them on the next, in Christ.

In the sixth chapter of St John's Gospel, Jesus explains that God's great gift of life to the world centres on the mysterious gift of Jesus himself to us as food and drink, in what we now call the Eucharist:

> In all truth I tell you, it was not Moses who gave you the bread from heaven, it is my Father who gives you the bread from heaven, the true bread; for the bread of God is the bread which comes down from heaven and gives life to the world... In all truth I tell you, everyone who believes has eternal life. I am the bread of life... Whoever eats my flesh and drinks my blood lives in me and I live in that person. As the living Father sent me and I draw life from the Father, so whoever eats me will also draw life from me. (Jn 6:32-33; 47-48; 56-57)

These are not easy words! John tells us that many of Jesus' followers could not accept them and left. Nevertheless, Jesus insisted, 'The words I have spoken to you are spirit and they are life' (*Jn* 6:63). We must ponder them carefully. First of all, we see that the constant theme is 'life'. Life is what Jesus and his words are all about. Then we note that Jesus seems to be describing himself as a 'life-line' for us. He says that he himself clings to the

Father and draws life from him, and that we ourselves can, in turn, cling to him (Jesus) and draw life from him, through eating and drinking what he gives us, his own body and blood. The net effect is that, in Christ, through the Eucharist, we ourselves can draw life from the one source of all life, namely God the Father.

From all eternity, the Father gives life in the blessed Trinity to the Son and the Holy Spirit. Father, Son and Spirit live in a communion of life which is everlasting because it is uncreated, it had no beginning. Anything created had a beginning and has life only as a gift; it can therefore die if that gift is taken away. Its hold on life is fragile. So Christ himself, the Son of God, in his created humanity could die and did die, but he clung all along to his heavenly Father ('Father, into your hands I commit my spirit', *Lk* 23:46) and the Father raised him in triumph by the power of the Spirit. St Paul teaches that that same wonder will be worked in us: 'if the Spirit of him who raised Jesus from the dead has made his home in you, then he who raised Christ Jesus from the dead will give life to your own mortal bodies through his Spirit living in you' (*Rom* 8:11).

The Church is sent to proclaim that Christ is risen and that life has conquered death. Since that life is given to us as food and drink in the Eucharist, it follows that the Eucharist plays a decisive role in the life of the Church. It has a programmatic role; it sets the tone for everything else. The Second Vatican Council expressed this great truth by simply saying that the eucharistic sacrifice is 'the source and summit of the Christian life' (Dogmatic Constitution on the Church, *Lumen Gentium,* hereafter *LG,* 11).[2] A famous pioneer of Vatican II, the French Jesuit, Henri de Lubac, coined the famous phrase that: 'the Eucharist makes the Church',[3] and in the same line of thought

> *The Eucharist makes the Church*

Cardinal Joseph Ratzinger has said: 'The Church is the celebration of the Eucharist; the Eucharist is the Church; they do not simply stand side by side; they are one and the same; it is from there that everything else radiates.'[4] Likewise the *Catechism of the Catholic Church* (*CCC*) teaches: '"The Church" is the People that God gathers in the whole world. She exists in local communities and is made real as a liturgical, above all a Eucharistic, assembly.' (*CCC* 752)

Our Orthodox and Eastern Catholic brothers and sisters always highlight the vital role of the Holy Spirit in the life of Jesus and in the life of the Church, while sadly we in the West are often rather inattentive to the Spirit. So let us emphasise straight away that, just as Jesus was raised to life by the Father in the power of the Spirit (cf *Rom* 8:11), so the Church celebrates the Eucharist by the power of the same Spirit, and lives in 'the fellowship of the Holy Spirit' (*2 Cor* 13:13). In the Creed, we proclaim that the Spirit is 'the Lord, the giver of life', and there is an *epiclesis,* an invocation of the Spirit, that accompanies the words of consecration in the Mass: e.g. 'Let your Spirit come upon these gifts to make them holy, so that they may become for us the body and blood of our Lord, Jesus Christ' (Eucharistic Prayer II). The international Catholic-Orthodox ecumenical dialogue has spoken very clearly about the role of the Spirit in the Eucharist and in the Church. 'The Spirit *transforms* the sacred gifts into the Body and Blood of Christ (*metabole,* change) in order to bring about the growth of the Body which is the Church.' In fact, it says, the entire celebration of the Eucharist is an *epiclesis,* which simply becomes more explicit at certain moments. All in all: 'The Church is continually in a state of epiclesis.'[5]

Epiclesis: Invocation of the Holy Spirit, e.g. Let your Spirit come upon these gifts to make them holy

2. SACRIFICE

Jesus was raised to life on a Sunday, the first day of the week, and the Church consequently celebrates every Sunday as the day of Resurrection, the day of new life, the Day of the Lord (*Dies Domini*),[6] a mini-Easter. Though we can celebrate the Eucharist every day, Sunday has always been the main day for its celebration, and the Church urges us to take part in the celebration not just as an obligation but as a regular renewal of Easter grace and Easter joy amid the difficulties and struggles of life. The Eucharist is like a sure compass in our hand, and this regular celebration keeps us on the right track by 'making us take our bearings from the victory of life'.[7]

> *The Eucharist has always been the celebration of the life which conquers death*

Just as there would be nothing to celebrate about Christ's death if he had not been raised (*1 Cor* 15:12-19), so there would, of course, be no Resurrection without Calvary. The Eucharist has always been the celebration of the life which conquers death, and therefore of the Father's supremely loving response to Christ's supremely loving *sacrifice*. At the heart of the Eucharist is the sacrifice of Jesus: 'When we eat this bread and drink this cup, we proclaim your death, Lord Jesus, until you come in glory' (memorial acclamation, cf *1 Cor* 11:26). As Pope John Paul has recently taught, the Mass is the 'sacramental re-presentation of Christ's sacrifice, crowned by the resurrection'.[8]

This sacrifice is 'so decisive for the salvation of the human race that Jesus Christ offered it and returned to the Father only *after he had left us a means of sharing in it* as if we had been present there'.[9] When Jesus died, there were those who passed by and mocked (*Mt* 27:39-40). Presumably, there were also others who simply watched as spectators. The centurion had the beginnings of understanding of what was really happening (*Mt* 27:54), but the full understanding has been entrusted to the Church. We know that Jesus died for the salvation of the world (*Jn* 3:16-17). It is therefore our own deepest desire not simply to be spectators of what was happening on Calvary, but to be participants, to enter into and share what Jesus was doing, and that is precisely what he made possible at the Last Supper. He established a doorway into the mystery of his sacrifice. By eating and drinking what he gave them there, his disciples already participated in his passion. 'The institution of the Eucharist sacramentally anticipated the events which were about to take place, beginning with the agony in Gethsemane.'[10] The Mass is the re-enactment of the Last Supper in accordance with Jesus' instruction: 'do this in remembrance of me' (*Lk* 22:19; *1 Cor* 11:24-25). By eating and drinking what the Lord gives us, we too enter into the mystery of his sacrifice, as if passing through a doorway. The Mass marvellously enables us still today to accompany Jesus on the journey he took from the upper room and to participate in the mystery of his suffering and death. However, we celebrate knowing the glorious outcome of that journey, we celebrate his sacrifice 'crowned by the resurrection',[11] the entire Paschal Mystery, so our remembrance is shot through with Easter light. The lighted candles that we always have on or beside the altar for the celebration of Mass are a reminder of this; each is a mini-Paschal Candle.

Around five hundred years B.C., the four songs of the Suffering Servant were composed in the book of the prophet Isaiah (*Is* 42:1-9; 49:1-6; 50:4-11; 52:13-53:12). These songs have a special place in the Church's Holy Week liturgy. In Isaiah's description of the Servant who turns out to be the saviour, Christians recognise the features of Christ himself, who was exposed to insult and spittle (*Is* 50:6) and crushed in the eyes of the world (*Is* 53:5), but whose suffering had an astonishing outcome. Like the faithful Servant, he was upheld by God (*Is* 42:1) and established as 'covenant of the people and light to the nations' (*Is* 42:6; 49:6), bringing salvation to the ends of the earth (*Is* 49:6).

The celebration that Jesus held with his friends on the eve of his passion already contained important references to the songs of the Servant. We have four accounts in the New Testament of the Last Supper (*Mt* 26:26-29; *Mk* 14:22-25; *Lk* 22:15-20; *1 Cor* 11:23-26),[12] and all of them report that Jesus referred to the 'covenant', the bond of unity that God forges with his people, as he gave the cup to his friends: 'this is my blood, the blood of the covenant, poured out for many' (*Mt* 26:28; *Mk* 14:24); 'this cup is the new covenant in my blood' (*Lk* 22:20; *1 Cor* 11:25); and the reference to the 'many' is itself taken from the fourth song: 'my servant will justify many by taking their guilt on himself' (*Is* 53:11).

Faithful Jews had waited hundreds of years longing for the Servant to be revealed and longing for the salvation he would bring to them and to the whole world. He would clearly be one of them, and his solidarity with the people would enable a marvellous exchange, he would take their guilt upon himself and by his bruises would bring healing to all (*Is* 53:5). He would *embody* their salvation. On Good Friday, Jesus was revealed as the Servant on Calvary, living to the last in fidelity to God. On Easter Sunday, having been upheld by God, he was established as light of the nations. But how can we

We have four accounts in the New Testament of the Last Supper (Mt 26:26-29; Mk 14:22-25; Lk 22:15-20; 1 Cor 11:23-26)

claim a part in the salvation he has won? The answer lies in what he already did on the evening of Holy Thursday, when he instituted the Eucharist. Those three days therefore form the most intense unity, and we celebrate them as a unity, the 'Easter Triduum'. As the faithful Servant, Jesus instituted the Eucharist not just in anticipation of his sacrifice on Good Friday, but also totally trusting that God would uphold him and raise him up, such that 'the whole *Triduum paschale*... is as it were gathered up, foreshadowed and "concentrated" for ever in the gift of the Eucharist'.[13]

3. COMMUNION

Sin cuts us off from God and from one another. Jesus died 'to gather together into one the scattered children of God' (*Jn* 11:52). The fruit of his sacrifice is therefore our unity, or *communion,* both with God and with each other. That is why the Eucharist, which celebrates and renews, but never repeats, the sacrifice of Christ, is so deeply linked to the Church, the family of all those reconciled with God and with one another as brothers and sisters in Christ.[14] The Eucharist makes the Church to be what it is, a great 'sacrament', both 'sign and instrument' of communion with God and of unity among all people (cf *LG* 1).

The bond between being reconciled with God and being reconciled with one another is a very rich one. God himself is the Trinity, the communion of Father, Son and Holy Spirit. Jesus is the Son made man for us, and the life he comes to share with us is God's life, the life of total and perfect communion. Those who are baptised into Christ are therefore baptised into communion, and the Church itself is called to be an image or icon of the Trinity. We see therefore the great significance of the fact that receiving the Eucharist is called receiving 'Holy Communion'. The Eucharist renews the gift of our Baptism, as we saw earlier, and the life that we are receiving and renewing there is the communion life of God himself. It follows that, even though we receive the Eucharist individually, it is really *communities* and *the whole Church* that Christ is feeding. The Eucharist makes the Church. So we should be conscious of those with whom we receive; by receiving together we are really undertaking to bear witness together to the unity and peace of the Trinity.

That is why those who are about to receive exchange a sign of peace. The message is that those who are not prepared to be reconciled if they have been at odds with one another cannot proceed to receive the Eucharist. The Eucharist is about reconciliation. No disputes should emerge from the celebration of the Eucharist still intact. That is what Jesus teaches when he says: 'if you are bringing your offering to the altar and there remember that your brother has something against you, leave your offering there before the altar, go and be reconciled with your brother first, and then come back and present your offering' (*Mt* 5:23-24).

4. Body of Christ and People of God

There are many names for the Church, and images of its communion life, e.g the vine and the branches (*Jn* 15:1-5), 'living stones making a spiritual house' (*1 Pet* 2:4-5). Two of the greatest images are those of the Body of Christ (cf *LG* 7) and the People of God (cf *LG*, chapter 2). Both of these images have very strong roots in the Eucharist and can help us to appreciate the significance of the fact that we use both bread and wine in the Mass.

The image of the Body of Christ comes exclusively from St Paul and undoubtedly originates in his conversion on the road to Damascus. A bright light shone, he fell to the ground and heard a voice saying: 'Saul, Saul, why are you persecuting me?', and again, 'I am Jesus, whom you are persecuting' (*Acts* 9:3-5). It was actually Jesus' followers that Saul was persecuting, but he suddenly realised that Jesus is risen and that he lives in his followers, so that to lay hands upon them is actually laying hands upon him ('Why are you persecuting *me?*'). Jesus is really and tangibly present in them; they are his body, the Body of Christ. Paul himself was baptised and gradually discovered this mystery in his own person: 'I am alive; yet it is no longer I, but Christ living in me' (*Gal* 2:20). The self-same mystery unites all Christians with one another, so that all are 'parts of one another' (*Eph* 4:25; cf *Rom* 12:5).

Paul gives a lot of teaching on this great theme in his first letter to the Corinthians (e.g *1 Cor* 12:12-30) and it is no coincidence that this is the letter in which he gives one of the four accounts we have of the institution of the Eucharist (*1 Cor* 11:23-26). He himself makes the connection between the Eucharist and the Church when he says: 'The blessing-cup, which we bless, is it not a sharing (*koinonia*) in the blood of Christ; and the loaf of bread which we break, is it not a sharing (*koinonia*) in the body of Christ?' (*1 Cor* 10:16). Paul's Greek word, *koinonia,* is often translated into English simply as 'communion', but it primarily means 'participation', so Paul's teaching here has layers of meaning. First of all, by means of the bread and the cup we participate in the body and blood of Christ himself, but then also, participating together in Christ produces a profound communion between ourselves, so our 'sharing' has both a vertical and also a horizontal dimension.

> *By receiving the bread which has become Christ's body, we ourselves are united in his Body which is the Church*

He then adds: 'And as there is one loaf, so we, although there are many of us, are one single body, for we all share in the one loaf' (*1 Cor* 10:17). In short, 'one bread, one body'.[15] At the Last Supper, Jesus took bread, gave thanks, broke it and said: 'This is my body' (*Mt* 26:26; *Mk* 14:22;

Lk 22:19; *1 Cor* 11:24). Clearly, Paul understands that, by receiving the bread which has become Christ's body, we ourselves are united in his Body which is the Church. In other words, we receive the body of Christ in order to become the Body of Christ. This is one of the main lines of scriptural reflection associated with our use of bread for the celebration of the Eucharist.

What, then, of the wine? We have already seen that Jesus links the cup to the covenant and thereby recalls the prophetic figure of the Suffering Servant. But there are, in fact, further strands of meaning that converge upon the cup from the Old Testament by means of the mention of covenant. It's helpful to remember what happened in the desert at Mount Sinai, when God made a covenant with his people through Moses.

Moses went and told the people all Yahweh s words and all the laws, and all the people answered with one voice, All the words Yahweh has spoken we will carry out! Moses put all Yahweh s words into writing, and early next morning he built an altar at the foot of the mountain, with twelve standing-stones for the twelve tribes of Israel. Then he sent certain young Israelites to offer burnt offerings and sacrifice bullocks to Yahweh as communion sacrifices. Moses then took half the blood and put it into basins, and the other half he sprinkled on the altar. Then, taking the Book of the Covenant, he read it to the listening people, who then said, We shall do everything

> that Yahweh has said; we shall obey. Moses then took the
> blood and sprinkled it upon the people, saying, This is the
> blood of the covenant which Yahweh has made with you,
> entailing all these stipulations. (*Ex* 24:3-8)

Certain words and phrases (e.g. 'communion', 'blood of
the covenant') immediately strike us in this account
because they are part of the fabric of Christian life and
liturgy. We see that they originate in the faith of Israel
where the roots of Christianity lie. Moreover, the
sequence of this solemn gathering of the People of God in
the desert is very like the basic structure of the Mass, in
two parts: the Liturgy of the Word and then the Liturgy of
the Eucharist. A comparison between the gathering and
the Mass is very instructive. The terms of the covenant
were proclaimed to the people and they expressed the
desire to respond and to be in communion with this God,
therefore sacrifices must be offered. Likewise, the Liturgy
of the Word and particularly the Gospel in the Mass
proclaim to us afresh the terms of the new and everlasting
covenant and we ourselves are invited to renew our
commitment to it through communion with God in the
sacrifice of Christ. That sacrifice took place once and for
all (*Rom* 6:10; *Heb* 7:27; 10:10) on Calvary and can never
be repeated, but having taken place there it is now
engraved in the heavens, as we shall see, and overarches
time, so that all of history can be drawn into it. The

Israelites went to find offerings; we bring forward bread and wine in a procession of gifts that expresses the response in our hearts.

Let us focus on the wine. By the power of the Holy Spirit, it is transformed into the blood of Christ. As we have seen, at the Last Supper, Jesus gave the cup to his friends to drink and said to them: 'this is my blood of the covenant' (*Mt* 26:28; *Mk* 14:24; *RSV*). There is both continuity and discontinuity here between the Old and New Testaments. The idea of 'blood of the covenant' is inherited from of old, but the fact that this blood should now be *Christ's own* blood is utterly *new*. The other two Last Supper accounts emphasise this newness by actually reporting Jesus as saying: 'This cup is the new covenant in my blood' (*Lk* 22:20; *1 Cor* 11:25). In fact, yet another strand of prophecy is to be woven in here, for the expression 'new covenant' comes from Jeremiah:

> Look, the days are coming, Yahweh declares, when I shall make a new covenant with the House of Israel (and the House of Judah), but not like the covenant I made with their ancestors the day I took them by the hand to bring them out of Egypt, a covenant which they broke, even though I was their Master, Yahweh declares. No, this is the covenant I shall make with the House of Israel when those days have come, Yahweh declares. Within them I shall plant my Law, writing it on their hearts. Then I shall be their God and they will be my people (Jer 31:31-33).

God foretells the final establishment of his people in a completely new intimacy of relationship. The Law would no longer be written on tablets of stone but upon their hearts. Accordingly, when Jesus established the new covenant, he did so not in the blood of animals but in his own blood, and the blood was no longer thrown over the people but drunk deep within. So, the wine we present in the Mass becomes the blood of Christ, and when we receive the blood of Christ, 'the blood of the new and everlasting covenant', we should recall the ancient roots of what we are doing. From earliest times, the People of God has been a covenant people, formed as a people by a covenant that was solemnly ratified in blood. That ancient ritual was given a new and definitive form by Christ at the Last Supper, and now today in the Mass, by giving us the blood of Christ, God is fashioning his people in its new and definitive form. This is one of the main lines of scriptural reflection associated with our use of wine for the celebration of the Eucharist.

Our celebration of the Mass with both bread and wine is therefore full of scriptural résonances that help us to realise that it is the Church as a community, the Body of Christ and the People of God, that is being fed and built up when we receive the body and blood of Christ. The bread becomes his body and the wine his blood, and it is clearly good to receive communion under both kinds, that way we can better heed all the resonances. 'The sign of communion is more complete when given under both kinds, since in that form the sign of the eucharistic meal appears more clearly. The intention of Christ that the new and eternal covenant be ratified in his blood is better expressed, as is the relation of the eucharistic banquet to the heavenly banquet.'[16] However, we must always remember that the Church teaches that we receive Christ entirely, body, blood, soul and divinity, even when we receive communion only under one kind.[17]

5. BODY AND BLOOD

It is easy for Christians who are well used to the language of the Eucharist to fail to realise how shocking it is at first sight. We eat the body of Christ and drink his blood! It is vital to have a proper grasp of what this actually means, both for an effective catechesis inside the Church and also to help our explanations to those outside. With the benefit of our scriptural discussion so far, we are now in a position to understand the true meaning of this language by setting it in a scriptural context.

Though the New Testament was written in Greek, its mindset is Hebrew. The Greek word for 'body' in all the Last Supper accounts is *soma,* but the proper understanding of it is not according to the Greek scheme by which a human being consists of 'body and soul'. We ourselves tend to understand 'body' as the Greeks did, as only *part* of a human being, the material, visible bit, but that is not the Hebrew meaning, so it is of no use in helping us to understand what Jesus said at the Last Supper. Jesus and the apostles were Jews, and 'body' in the Hebrew understanding does not just mean the outer aspect of a human being, something they *have,* rather it means what a human being *is*. Soma is 'the nearest equivalent to our word "personality"'; *soma* is 'the whole person'.[18] So, when Jesus says to his friends, 'This is my body', he means 'This is myself, my whole being', and he gives himself to them so that they, by receiving, will in fact be drawn into his own self-gift to his Father, and will be drawn to one another in his self-gift.

Blood also has a very specific significance in the Bible: 'the life of the creature is in the blood' (*Lev* 17:11). It was thought that the breath was in the blood, and hence life itself. Because life comes from God, blood was sacred as the very symbol of life. The flesh of animals could be consumed but never their blood, and the blood of animals that was shed in sacrifice symbolised the self-offering of the person sacrificing, the dedication of their own life to God.[19] So, when Jesus says to his friends, 'This is my blood', again he means 'This is myself, my very life'; the life that God gave him he, in turn, is giving to them so that his life might be in them and they, in him, might dwell in God.

There is undoubtedly, therefore, the most clear and profound identification of the bread and wine with Jesus himself. They are changed and become him. However, this change is not a static thing, to be marvelled at in itself. Rather, the whole setting of the Last Supper, and therefore of the Mass, is a dynamic one. Jesus transforms bread and wine, food and drink, into his body and blood, so that they will be eaten and drunk and that the recipients will thereby be drawn into his own sacrifice and 'enter into the movement of his self-offering'[20] to his Father. By doing so, they will also be drawn into union with one another, and ultimately they themselves will be transformed. As we saw above, we receive the body of Christ so as to become the Body of Christ. Vatican II quoted Pope St Leo the Great's magnificent statement of this truth: 'the sharing in the body and blood of Christ has no other effect than to accomplish our transformation into that which we receive'.[21]

> *We receive the body of Christ so as to become the Body of Christ*

Every sacrament is an encounter with Christ, the living Lord, and the effect of every sacrament is to build us up as members of his Body, the Church. The Church is the locus of all the sacraments, and is itself 'the great sacrament which contains and vitalises all the others'.[22] Vatican II not only speaks of the Church itself as a sacrament, as we have seen,[23] but it also relates each of the individual sacraments to the Church (cf *LG* 11). They are decisive moments in the life of the Church and of its members, when Christ himself acts to unite us with himself and with one another in him. When we say that they confer 'grace', this is not a commodity, that is being 'topped-up', it is our participation in the life of God himself as members of the Body of Christ, that is being strengthened and deepened.[24] This happens most of all in the Eucharist, where Christ actually gives himself to us, and the whole mystery of the Body of Christ is contained in what we receive. All of the other sacraments refer in some way to the Eucharist, that's why we often celebrate them (e.g. baptisms, confirmations, weddings, ordinations, anointings) in the context of the Mass. All of the sacraments transform us, but the Eucharist is the focal point of our transformation, because there we actually receive what we are being transformed into, namely, the Body of Christ.

It was the result of that transformation that Paul was made acutely aware of on the road to Damascus, when the risen Jesus asked him not, 'Why are you persecuting my scattered individual followers', but 'Why are you persecuting *me*'. Paul no doubt pondered the true meaning of those words for the rest of his life, and based much of his teaching on them. We can say that the presence of Christ in the Eucharist must be real when his presence in the Church that has received the Eucharist is as real as Paul discovered on the Damascus road. In other words, one of the strongest arguments for the real presence of Christ in the eucharistic elements of bread and wine is the reality of his presence in the Church which has received those elements. What Jesus basically said to Paul on the road was, 'the Church is me'. Likewise, what he basically said to his friends at the Last Supper about the bread and about the wine was, 'this is me'; and his presence in the elements and his presence in the Church are intimately linked. The *Catechism* describes the beautiful way in which Eastern liturgies express this link. The gifts are: *'Sancta sanctis!',* that is 'God's holy gifts for God's holy people' (*CCC* 948).

There is, perhaps, a deliberate ambiguity when Paul tells the Corinthians that 'a person who eats and drinks without recognising the body is eating and drinking his own condemnation' (*1 Cor* 11:29). He is referring immediately to the bread and the cup (cf v.27), Christ's body must be recognised there; but he seems to be referring also to the imperative of charity to fellow-members of the Church, who are also Christ's body (vv.20-22; 33-34). The body is to be recognised and honoured in both senses, and we are to examine our conscience carefully on both counts before receiving (v.28).

If we have a strong understanding of the Church itself as the Body of Christ, we will have no difficulty in acknowledging the bread and wine which nourish the Church as themselves the body and blood of Christ. Ecclesial realism and eucharistic realism support each other, said de Lubac: 'ecclesial realism ensures eucharistic realism', and vice-versa.[25]

6. Past, Present and Future

Every Mass is a memorial of the past and an anticipation of the future, a memorial of the death and Resurrection of the Lord and also an anticipation of the life of heaven. Vatican II taught that Christ instituted the Eucharist 'in order to perpetuate the sacrifice of the Cross throughout the ages until he should come again' (Constitution on the Sacred Liturgy, *Sacrosanctum Concilium,* hereafter *SC,* 47), and also that: 'In the earthly liturgy we take part in a foretaste of that heavenly liturgy which is celebrated in the Holy City of Jerusalem toward which we journey as pilgrims' (*SC* 8). These dramatic statements sound as if they will need to be treated separately because they seem to be referring to quite different aspects of the Mass, one looking backwards and one looking forwards. But it is not very satisfactory to have our understanding of the Mass divided into lots of different compartments. It is one and the same celebration, so can these aspects not somehow be held together? Yes they can, and the Letter to the Hebrews gives a clue as to how.

What you have come to is nothing known to the senses... What you have come to is Mount Zion and the city of the living God, the heavenly Jerusalem where the millions of angels have gathered for the festival, with the whole Church of the first-born, enrolled as citizens of heaven. You have come to God himself, the supreme Judge, and to the spirits of the upright who have been made perfect; and to Jesus the mediator of a new covenant, and to purifying blood which pleads more insistently than Abel s. (Heb 12:18; 22-24; amended trans.)

This sounds very odd at first! We need to remember that the letters of the New Testament were received not by individuals to be read over breakfast, but by Christian communities to be read when the community was gathered, and the weekly assembly took place on the first day of the week, the Lord's Day, for the Eucharist, the breaking of bread (cf *Acts* 20:7-12). The Letter to the Hebrews seems to have been written from Italy (*Heb* 13:24) to a community of Jewish converts to Christianity, hence 'to the Hebrews'. Secondly, it was written to lift their spirits. It seems that these converts had moved away from Jerusalem and from the splendour of worship in the Temple for fear of persecution, and were downcast. The author himself could have imagined the circumstances in which they would read the letter, perhaps in a modest upper room, locked for safety, with just a few people present. He knew that, as they looked around them, that is what they would see, that was what it *appeared* they had come to. So he wrote in order to help them see more fully what was truly happening. Hence he starts, 'What you have come to', i.e. what you have *really* come to, if only you would realise. Wherever and whenever we celebrate the Mass, and whatever the appearances are, these words give us the proper perspective. There is more to the Mass than meets the eye!

The scene he describes is full of wonder! It is a gathering in the heavenly Jerusalem, so his implication is that the participants shouldn't pine for the earthly Jerusalem. Furthermore, it seems that they are having a foretaste of the *final* gathering there on the last day, because there is mention of the Judge and of Christ himself making intercession with the power of his saving blood. There is a full assembly of angels and saints, all of the first-born are present, and the assembly bears the name 'Church' (*'ekklesia'* in Greek). This word literally means 'assembly'. Since Jesus died 'to gather together into one the scattered children of God' (*Jn* 11:52), it follows that the final achievement of his work will be the great gathering that he assembles; the Gathering, with a capital 'G', the Assembly, with a capital 'A', i.e. the Church, with a capital 'C'. The Church, properly speaking, is that future final assembly, as the *Catechism* teaches: 'The Church is the goal of all things' (*CCC* 760).

The Letter to the Hebrews therefore teaches that, when we gather for the earthly liturgy, even in very humble circumstances, that great final heavenly gathering breaks upon us. We are lifted up into it, and have a foretaste of the 'heavenly liturgy which is celebrated in the Holy City of Jerusalem toward which we journey as pilgrims' (*SC* 8). Moreover, we note that at the centre of that heavenly assembly stands Jesus with his precious and purifying blood, mediating the new covenant. In other words, Calvary has not been forgotten. The Letter to the Hebrews shows that it never will be

> *In the Mass we have a foretaste of the 'heavenly liturgy'*

forgotten. Christ's once and for all sacrifice is now engraved in the heavens; it overarches history, and for all eternity we shall celebrate the victory won on Calvary and sing with the angels, 'Worthy is the Lamb that was sacrificed to receive power, riches, wisdom, strength, honour, glory and blessing' (*Rev* 5:12). Precisely by being a foretaste of the heavenly Jerusalem, therefore, the Mass celebrated by the Church on earth perpetuates the sacrifice of the Cross throughout the ages 'until he should come again' (*SC* 47).

The *Sanctus* in every Mass, 'Holy, holy, holy', is a powerful reminder that we are being lifted up to join in the heavenly praise: 'And so, with all the choirs of angels in heaven we proclaim your glory and join in their unending hymn of praise...'.[26] The prophet, Isaiah, heard 'Holy, holy, holy' being sung by the seraphim around God's throne in the vision he had when he was called (*Is* 6:3), and John hears it again, being sung by the four living creatures around the throne, in the visions he records in the Book of Revelation (*Rev* 4:8). These visions reinforce the uplifting message of the Letter to the Hebrews. No doubt that is why both writings have been treasured and passed down by the Church all through the ages, as a remedy against the constant danger of becoming downcast and burdened by the cares of the world. John himself says that he saw his visions on 'the Lord's day' (*Rev* 1:10), when he would presumably have been celebrating the Eucharist, and we recall that the writer of the Letter to the Hebrews was himself wanting to open up a fuller vision of what is happening in the Eucharist. There are striking similarities in what they describe. The Spirit took hold of John (*Rev* 1:10), and he too saw 'the holy city, the new Jerusalem, coming down out of heaven from God' (*Rev* 21:2), and a mighty gathering: 'a huge number, impossible for anyone to count, of people from every nation, race, tribe and language; they were standing in front of the throne and in front of the Lamb' (*Rev* 7:9). Again, we can note the crucial point that Calvary has not been forgotten, for the Lamb was 'standing, as though it had been slain' (*Rev* 5:6; *RSV*), in other words still bearing the marks of the passion, no longer as wounds but as trophies of victory: 'I am the Living One, I was dead and look - I am alive for ever and ever, and I hold the keys of death and of Hades' (*Rev* 1:17-18). Again, we appreciate that the Gospel is primarily about the victory of Christ over death.

In the Eucharist, Christ proclaims this good news once again to his people, shares his risen life with us, and so gives us *hope* for the future. In every Mass, we ourselves are evangelised and renewed, so that we, in our turn, may go out to share the good news with others, ready to give an account of the hope that is in us (*1 Pet* 3:15).

7. THE UNFOLDING STORY

We have seen that there are, in fact, three meanings that the term 'Body of Christ' can have. It could refer to Christ himself, to the Eucharist, or to the Church. All of these meanings are richly interlinked. The history of the Church shows that different periods have been particularly preoccupied with different aspects of these links. Broadly speaking, we can say that the first millennium, the period of the Church Fathers, was particularly fascinated by the link between the Eucharist and the Church, and studied the way in which the Eucharist builds community and gives shape to the Church's life, whereas the second millennium, the scholastic era, largely as a result of doctrinal challenges of various sorts, was particularly preoccupied with the link between Christ himself and the Eucharist, and studied the way in which Christ is really present under the forms of bread and wine.

The Second Vatican Council, on the threshold of the third millennium, restored much of the focus on the *ecclesial* and community dimension of the Eucharist that the Fathers loved to explain in their homilies and writings; this holy sacrament, it taught, 'aptly signifies and admirably realises' the 'unity of the People of God' (*LG* 11). The Eucharist is the sacrament 'from which the

Church ever derives its life and on which it thrives' (*LG* 26).[27] The link between the Church and the Eucharist has also been a major topic in the ecumenical dialogue of recent decades, in which the Catholic Church has played a full part.[28] Let us see some of the main points in the unfolding story.

8. THE FIRST MILLENNIUM

Parishes were formed in the fourth and fifth centuries when the number of Christians became so large, especially after the Emperor Constantine and his successors ended the persecution of the Church and embraced Christianity, that bishops could no longer gather all of their people together in one place and minister to them. Prior to that time, in each locality, the whole community would generally gather with their bishop for the weekly Eucharist and he would preside. It was understood that the Eucharist is the central act in the Church's life, the celebration that makes the Church what it is, and therefore it was obvious that the bishop, who is charged to shepherd and build up the Church, would himself preside at the Eucharist.

a. St Ignatius of Antioch (c.35 - c.107)

Just as St Paul was concerned about factions in Corinth (*1 Cor* 1:10), so St Ignatius was concerned about factions in the local churches that he wrote to while on his long journey to Rome to be martyred. He told the people of Smyrna: 'Abjure all factions, for they are the beginning of evils'. In particular, Christians should not split into factions to celebrate the Eucharist just with their family or friends. 'The sole Eucharist you should consider valid is one that is celebrated by the bishop himself, or by some person authorised by him. Where the bishop is to be seen, there let all his people be; just as wherever Jesus Christ is present, we have the catholic Church.'[29] This is the first time that the expression,

The eucharistic bread is: 'the medicine of immortality'

'the catholic Church', is mentioned in Christian literature. Ignatius clearly understands the people gathered around their bishop for the Eucharist as a portrayal of the final heavenly scene of the multitudes gathered around the throne of God and the Lamb, as described in the Letter to the Hebrews and the Book of Revelation. This passage from Ignatius was one of the key texts cited by Vatican II when it explained the role of the bishop among his people. The bishop is primarily the 'High Priest', presider at the local church's liturgy (*SC* 41), not just a governing figure, and the Church itself is a family of local eucharistic churches 'under the sacred ministry of the bishop' (*LG* 26).

Likewise, Ignatius urged the Ephesians 'to share in the one common breaking of bread', and he then gave a wonderful description of what the eucharistic bread is: 'the medicine of immortality, and the sovereign remedy by which we escape death and live in Jesus Christ for evermore'.[30] Uppermost in his mind was clearly the victory of Christ over death and the share we are given in that victory by receiving the Eucharist. The Eucharist is 'the one common breaking of bread' by which, together with one another, we 'live in Christ for evermore'. In short, therefore, the Eucharist makes the Church.

Ignatius was particularly concerned about the harmful influence of Docetism, a heresy which maintained that the incarnation, passion and resurrection of Jesus were all just an appearance rather than reality. This view made him angry, particularly since he himself was, in full reality, on his way to martyrdom! 'After all', he wrote, 'if everything our Lord did was only illusion, then these chains of mine must be illusory too!'[31] In actual fact, he stressed, Jesus himself was 'truly pierced', he died and was truly raised. He appeared to Peter and his companions and 'ate and drank with them after He was risen, like any natural man, even though He and the Father were spiritually one'.[32] Ignatius' teaching on the realism of the Eucharist is then crystal-clear. He praised the Smyrnaeans: 'I have seen how immovably settled in faith you are; nailed body and soul, as it were, to the cross of the Lord Jesus Christ, and rooted and grounded in love by His blood'.[33] The Docetists, in contrast, 'absent themselves from the Eucharist and the public prayers, because they will not admit that the Eucharist is the self-same body of our Saviour Jesus Christ which suffered for our sins, and which the Father in His goodness afterwards raised up again'.[34]

b. The 'Apostolic Tradition' (c.215?)

In the early twentieth century, scholars identified a manuscript as the long-lost *Apostolic Tradition,* believed to have been written around the year 215 in Rome by Hippolytus (c.170 - c.236), a presbyter who unfortunately became the first anti-pope, when he was elected as a rival bishop of Rome to Callistus. The manuscript gives an extremely important account of the liturgy and organisation of the early Church, and it duly became one of the principal resources for modern liturgical reform in many different Christian traditions. It was cited by Vatican II and is the source for our second Eucharistic Prayer, introduced after the Council. Unfortunately, the manuscript is a later translation, we don't have the original version of the text, and there is a strong possibility that it is, in fact, a composite document, with parts dating from the second, third and fourth centuries.[35] Nevertheless, it is a precious record of the life and worship of the early Christians.

The text contains ordination prayers for bishops, presbyters and deacons and these prayers contain a job description which enables us to understand what the various ministers did in the early Church. The prayer for a bishop, which was actually used in order to revise the Catholic ordination prayer for a bishop after Vatican II, asks God: enable the person you have chosen 'to feed your holy flock and to exercise the high priesthood for you without blame, ministering day and night; unceasingly to propitiate your countenance, and to offer you the holy gifts of your church'.[36]

We see once again, as we did from the letters of Ignatius, that the bishop was the presider at the community's Eucharist, offering the gifts. He was a priestly figure, not just an administrator, and when Vatican II taught that becoming a bishop was in fact being ordained to 'the high priesthood' (*LG* 21), it was the *Apostolic Tradition* that it referred to in a footnote as evidence. Of course, the title of 'High Priest' comes from the Letter to the Hebrews and refers to Christ himself (e.g. *Heb* 4:14), so when it was used by the early Church to refer to the bishop it meant that he, first and foremost, was the representative and image of Christ in the midst of his people, feeding them and making intercession for them before God.

> *The passion of our Lord is the sacrifice we offer*

c. St Cyprian (martyred, 258)

St Cyprian, who became a Christian only in 246, and then a bishop in 248, exercised his ministry in turbulent and dangerous times of persecution. We have many of his letters, and we find in them a moving testimony to the power of the Eucharist to sustain our Christian witness, even to the point of martyrdom. He stresses that 'the passion of our Lord is the sacrifice we offer',[37] and gives the first evidence we have of the Eucharist being offered daily and not just on Sundays when he refers to the bishops as: 'priests who offer up each day the sacrifices of God'.[38]

A famous line from Cyprian was quoted by Vatican II when it spoke of the Church's unity: the universal Church is 'a people brought into unity from the unity of the Father, the Son and the Holy Spirit' (*LG* 4).[39] Cyprian believed that the Eucharist is the sacrament of the Church's unity. He used the image of the loaf and said: 'just as numerous grains are gathered, ground, and mixed all together to make into one loaf of bread, so in Christ, who is the bread of heaven, we know there is but one body and that every one of us has been fused together and made one with it'.[40]

Under the pressure of persecution, some Christians had renounced their faith and offered sacrifice to the pagan gods. If they repented, a long period of penance was imposed, during which time they were denied the Eucharist, i.e. they were excommunicated. Seeing that a new persecution was imminent, however, Cyprian and his fellow bishops made a pastoral decision to reconcile these people as a matter of urgency, so that they could receive the Eucharist again and be strengthened by it.

> Those whom we stir and rouse to battle we must not leave all naked and unarmed; we must fortify and protect them with the body and blood of Christ. Since the

Eucharist has been appointed for this purpose, to be a safeguard to those who receive it, those whom we would have safe against the Enemy we must now arm with the protection of the Lord s banquet. How, I ask, are we to teach and incite them to shed their own blood by confessing the Name of Christ, of we deny to them on the eve of going into battle the blood of Christ? How can we make them fit for the cup of martyrdom, if we do not first allow them the right of communion and admit them to drink, in the Church, the cup of the Lord? [41]

By granting reconciliation, he says, we are making ready 'sacrificial victims and offerings for God'.[42]

These are words of great power, and they provide us with a profound reflection on the significance of receiving the Lord's blood, in particular. We are reminded of Jesus' question to the sons of Zebedee, 'Can you drink the cup that I am going to drink?' (*Mt* 20:22). He was referring, of course, to the cup of his passion (cf *Mt* 26:39, 42) and simply inviting them to walk the path of fidelity to God with him. There is material here for the catechesis that is still needed in order to promote reception of Communion under both kinds in the Catholic Church. As we approach the eucharistic cup, we might well consider Jesus himself asking us the same question: 'Can you drink the cup that I am going to drink?' As we take the cup and drink, we are saying 'Yes, Lord', and renewing our discipleship. What is more, as Cyprian understood, now that Christ is risen, his blood gives us the all the strength we need to walk that journey. Taking the cup is therefore also an act of the utmost trust in him; he is indeed our strength, come what may.[43]

d. St Ambrose (c.339-397)

The period of 'mystagogy' which follows Easter in the Rite of Christian Initiation of Adults (RCIA) is inspired by the period of intense teaching about the sacraments that bishops, especially in the fourth century, would give in the week after Easter to the newly baptised, who were now participating in the Eucharist fully for the first time. One of the most famous sets of these homilies was preached by St Ambrose in Milan probably in 391. His homilies were particularly influential, not least in the later controversy surrounding Berengar (see below, section 9a), because of their focus on the words of Christ himself that the bishop or priest says over the bread and wine in the Mass. Ambrose clearly identified those words as words of *consecration,* when the bread and wine are changed into the body and blood of Christ. In fact, he spoke of the words as *creative.*

[B]efore the sacramental words are uttered this bread is nothing but bread. But at the consecration this bread becomes the body of Christ... [B]y what words is the consecration effected, and whose words are they? The words of the Lord Jesus. All that is said before are the words of the priest: Praise is offered to God, the prayer is offered up, petitions are made for the people, for kings, for all others. But when the moment comes for bringing the most holy sacrament into being, the priest does not use his own words any longer: he uses the words of Christ. Therefore, it is Christ s words that bring this sacrament into being. What is this word of Christ? It is the word by which all things were made. The Lord commanded and the heavens were made, the Lord commanded and the earth was made, the Lord commanded and the seas were made, the Lord commanded and all creatures came into being. See, then, how efficacious the word of Christ is. If, then, there is such power in the word of the Lord Jesus that things begin to exist which did not exist before, how much more powerful it is for changing what already existed into something else. [44]

We saw in section 1, above, that it is by the power of the Holy Spirit that the bread and wine are changed. We can now clearly say, with Ambrose, that that change happens at the word of Christ. We must recall that Jesus Christ was filled with the Spirit at every moment (e.g. *Lk* 1:35; 4:1; 10:21) and that his very name means 'the anointed one'. It would therefore be futile to ask whether it is by the invocation of the Holy Spirit *or* by the words of Christ that the consecration occurs. It occurs by means of *both*.

e. St Augustine (354 - 430)

Of both the Church and the Eucharist interchangeably, St Augustine exclaimed: 'O sacrament of devotion! O sign of unity! O bond of charity!'[45] He is the perfect exponent of the patristic principle that 'the Eucharist makes the Church'. His teaching on the Eucharist is vigorous and stimulating; he turns the tables and reverses perspectives so as to make his point. In short, as he sees it, to receive the body of Christ in the Eucharist is, in fact, to be received by him into his Body which is the Church. The body of Christ which we take into ourselves actually takes us out of ourselves into the communion of the Church. We might even say that the food that we eat eats us!

In his *Confessions,* Augustine gave a moving account of when he first came to know God and heard him say from on high: 'I am the food of the fully grown; grow and you will feed on me. And you will not change me into you like the food your flesh eats, but you will be changed into me'.[46] Then, rather echoing a theme of Cyprian, as we saw above, he reflected in one of his homilies on the fact that the Lord used bread for the Eucharist, and compared the process by which a loaf is made to the process by which people are initiated into the Church.

> The Body of Christ , you are told, and you answer Amen . Be members then of the Body of Christ that your Amen may be true. Why is this mystery accomplished

with bread? We shall say nothing of our own about it, rather let us hear the Apostle [Paul], who speaking of this sacrament says: We being many are one body, one bread. Understand and rejoice. Unity, devotion, charity! One bread: and what is this one bread? One body made up of many. Consider that the bread is not made of one grain alone, but of many. During the time of exorcism, you were, so to say, in the mill. At baptism you were wetted with water. Then the Holy Spirit came into you like the fire which bakes the dough. Be then what you see and receive what you are. [47]

Here again is a splendid image from the Fathers for our catechesis today. Augustine sees the eucharistic bread itself as a parable of the Church, many once-scattered people who have now been united by the water of Baptism and the fire of the Spirit in Confirmation. As Christ comes to us in the form of bread, we learn that he is actually feeding his Church at that moment. It follows that we receive him properly when we truly want to be part of the Church, being at peace with our brothers and sisters and really living with them as the Body of Christ in the world. In fact, Augustine's gaze extends further, to the life of heaven. Christ in the Eucharist is actually fashioning that heavenly gathering that is most truly 'the Church' (cf *Heb* 12:23), as we saw in section 6, above. Augustine says of the Eucharist, 'this food and drink ...

makes those by whom it is taken immortal and incorruptible, that is, the very society of saints, where there will be peace and full and perfect unity'.[48] The Eucharist is the sacrament 'by which the Church is now united',[49] he said, and Vatican II cited this passage when it taught about the profound unity of all the local churches of the world because of the one Eucharist that they all celebrate (*LG* 26).

9. THE SECOND MILLENNIUM

For the early Fathers, as for St Paul, the Church on earth was a family of local churches, a communion of communities, bound together by the charity that springs from the one Lord in the one Eucharist that they all shared. Also like St Paul, they tended to refer to the Church simply as the Body of Christ, or perhaps the 'true body' (*corpus verum*), not as the *mystical* body of Christ (*corpus mysticum*). In fact, they spoke of the sacraments as 'the mysteries', and especially of the Eucharist as the sacred mysteries, as we still sometimes do. It follows that the *Eucharist* is, technically speaking, the 'mystical body of Christ', which literally just means the body of Christ present under the signs and symbols of the Church's sacramental life, in this case, the forms of bread and wine. We nowadays tend to speak of the *Eucharist* as the *true* body of Christ, and of the *Church* as his *mystical* body. In other words, the terminology of the Fathers has been reversed! How did this happen? It happened in reaction to the teaching of one of the first scholastic theologians, Berengar of Tours.

a. Berengar (c.1010 - 1088)

Berengar didn't properly understand the teaching of the Fathers. When they called the Eucharist the *mystical* body of Christ, they did not for a moment doubt that Christ was *really* present. The term simply meant that he was present under the sacramental forms of bread and wine. However, Berengar could not hold these aspects together and said that Christ was present only mystically, not truly. In his book, *Corpus Mysticum* (1949), Henri de Lubac describes how the Church reacted momentously to this challenge, gradually changing its vocabulary to avoid any misunderstanding and stressing that the Eucharist is indeed the *real* body of Christ, which meant that the adjective 'mystical' came to be dropped when speaking of the Eucharist. For a while, Eucharist and Church were both called the real body of Christ (*corpus verum*), but to avoid confusion the adjective 'mystical' eventually attached itself to the Church; it began to be called the *mystical* body of Christ, and the reversal of the terminology was complete!

This doesn't sound too problematic until we realise that, whereas the Fathers' thought tended to flow naturally and smoothly from Christ through the Eucharist to the Church (the *corpus verum*), now the train of thought tended to stop short at the presence of Christ in the Eucharist itself, and the link between the Eucharist and the Church began to be neglected. What was now greatly studied was simply the way in which Christ was present in the Eucharist, under the forms of bread and wine. De Lubac comments that whereas the Eucharist had been 'the mystery to understand', it now became 'the miracle to believe'.[50] Confronted with such a miracle, people often felt unworthy to receive.

b. Fourth Lateran Council (1215)

Scholastic theologians began to use the idea of 'transubstantiation', in other words, the idea that the substance of the bread and wine is transformed into the substance of the body and blood of Christ in the Mass. This idea was used, in 1202, by Pope Innocent III (1198-1216) when he said that Christ 'transubstantiated the bread and wine into his body and blood', and stressed that this meant that in the sacrament of the altar there was the *truth* (*veritas*) of the body and blood of Christ, and not just an image (*imago*), an appearance (*species*) or a figure (*figura*) (*DS* 1502). There is something of an echo of the battle of Ignatius against the Docetists here. 'Transubstantiation' was duly sanctioned by the Fourth Lateran Council, which declared that the body and blood of Christ are 'truly contained in the sacrament of the altar under the forms of bread and wine' (*DS* 802), and it has become normative in Catholic teaching.[51]

Before considering the robust defence of this idea that was made by the Council of Trent, we should note that it was the Fourth Lateran Council that recommended that the faithful should receive the Eucharist at least at Easter each year, having duly confessed their sins. It stipulated that confession at least once a year was required of all who had reached the age of discernment (*DS* 812). In this way, the idea of 'Easter duties' began.

c. Council of Trent (1545 - 1563)

Not long after the Fourth Lateran Council, the Second Council of Lyon (1274) listed the Eucharist simply as one of the seven sacraments of the Church. The accent had clearly shifted from the view that 'the Eucharist makes the Church' to the idea that 'the Church makes the Eucharist'; in other words, the Eucharist was now just one of the sacred actions that the Church performed, and was no longer the act that itself shaped the Church into a communion of local churches. In fact, the Church was now being shaped as a juridical pyramid with the pope at the summit as 'Vicar of Christ', a title first used by Pope Innocent III.[52]

We have seen that there was a change in the way the Eucharist was understood around the beginning of the second millennium. The relationship between the Eucharist and Christ himself began to dominate, to the exclusion of the relationship between the Eucharist and the Church, that had been such a rich patristic theme. Cardinal Joseph Ratzinger comments that 'the centre of the oldest ecclesiology is the eucharistic assembly', and that 'extraordinarily complex' changes later occurred. There was an 'increasing distinction between sacrament and jurisdiction, between liturgy and administration'. In other words, bishops now became administrative figures and the Mass became the priests' job. 'Like any other society, the Church was now, in a certain sense, a juridical instrument', he says, though of course she was distinguished by having the sacraments. Nevertheless, 'the Eucharist was just one of these - one liturgical act among others, no longer the encompassing orbit and dynamic centre of ecclesial existence per se'. 'In consequence, the Eucharist itself was fragmented into a variety of loosely related rites: sacrifice, worship, cultic meal', and 'the linking of the whole sacramental event to the oneness of the crucified and risen Lord was overshadowed by the emergence of a plurality of separate sacrificial rites'.[53]

In short, the great emphasis on the *sacramental* aspect of the Eucharist, on how the bread and wine are indeed changed into the body and blood of Christ, had led to the *sacrificial* aspect of the Eucharist being treated *separately,* and this separation opened the way for a dangerous misunderstanding, namely that a repetition of the sacrifice of the Cross was occurring. One of the leading English Reformers, Thomas Cranmer (1489-1556), significantly complained that the two chief roots of 'popery' were 'the popish doctrine of transubstantiation' and that of 'the sacrifice and oblation of Christ made by the priest for the salvation of the quick and the dead'.[54] He clearly had the totally mistaken impression that, in the Mass, Christ becomes present and is then sacrificed again by the priest! This complete misapprehension of Catholic belief perhaps still continues in some quarters.

In order to eradicate any danger of such a misunderstanding, the sacramental and sacrificial aspects of the Eucharist need to be held strictly together, we need to see the Mass as a 'sacramental sacrifice'. This notion is very scriptural and comes straight out of the biblical texts we saw earlier, in section 6. We shall return to it in section 9d, below. For now, we must simply note that a hallmark of the treatment of the Eucharist in the few centuries prior to the Council of Trent and, in particular, at the Council itself, was a firm *separation* of the two aspects. Trent produced its *Decree on the Most Holy Sacrament of the Eucharist,* dealing especially with transubstantiation, in 1551, and its *Decree on the Most Holy Sacrifice of the Mass* in 1562, eleven years apart! These two decrees are fundamental reference points for the Catholic Church's understanding of the Eucharist. They contain unchangeable pieces of the overall picture of Catholic belief. However, as I have suggested, Trent itself, because of its division of the material, did not fit the pieces fully together.

The gist of the two decrees is to be found in the canons that were attached to them, summarising their teaching. Let us examine them in turn.[55] The first canon of the first decree, on the Eucharist as sacrament, declares:

> If anyone denies that in the most holy sacrament of the Eucharist there are contained truly, really and substantially, the body and blood of our lord Jesus Christ together with the soul and divinity, and therefore the whole Christ, but says that he is present in it only as in a sign or figure or by his power: let him be anathema [56]

This canon clearly teaches the *real presence* of Christ in the Eucharist, and the second canon specifies the nature of this presence.

> If anyone says that in the venerable sacrament of the eucharist the substance of the bread and wine remains together with the body and blood of our lord Jesus Christ, and denies that marvellous and unique change of the whole substance of the bread into the body, and of the whole substance of the wine into the blood, while only the appearance of bread and wine remains, a change which the catholic church most aptly calls transubstantiation: let him be anathema.

The key to this second canon is the idea of *change*. Trent rejects the idea that the substance of the bread and wine might remain 'together with' the body and blood of Christ, an idea known as 'consubstantiation' and associated with Martin Luther, and it insists on 'transubstantiation': there is a marvellous and unique *change* in the bread and wine. What is at stake here becomes clear if we recall the link made in section 5, above, between eucharistic realism and ecclesial realism. The Eucharist feeds the Church, and what we say about the Eucharist will be strongly indicative of what we believe about the Church and about God's purpose for humanity and the world at large. If we believe that God's purpose is to *transform* us, so that one day we ourselves will shine in Christ with all the glory that shone from him at his Transfiguration (*Mt* 17:1-8), then it follows that we will believe that the Eucharist we receive centres upon a *transformation* of the bread and wine into Christ himself (cf *CCC* 1000). The Catholic Church firmly believes, as scripture teaches, that 'the greatest and priceless promises have been lavished on us' so that we may truly 'share the divine nature' (*2 Pet* 1:4), and be *divinised*. Therefore, at the heart of Catholic belief stands

Our participation in the Eucharist already gives us a foretaste of Christ s transfiguration of our bodies: Just as bread that comes from the earth, after God s blessing has been invoked upon it, is no longer ordinary bread, but Eucharist, formed of two things, the one earthly and the other heavenly: so too our bodies, which partake of the Eucharist, are no longer corruptible, but possess the hope of resurrection (St Irenaeus) (CCC 1000).

a firm conviction that the bread and wine of the Eucharist are indeed themselves most deeply changed and transformed into Christ himself. Belief in that change is the key to believing that God's whole purpose in Christ is to make 'the whole of creation new' (*Rev* 21:5), as is proclaimed at the culmination of the Book of Revelation.

On the other hand, belief in divinisation, or *'theosis'*, has not generally been associated with Luther. For him, the Christian was *simul iustus et peccator,* justified but still a sinner, and this tallies with a belief that, in the Eucharist, Christ is indeed really present, but there is still the substance of the bread and wine. Recent research which may revise our understanding of Luther's views on divinisation is of considerable ecumenical importance.[57] What is plain from Trent is the Catholic conviction that there is a *real change* in the bread and wine at Mass.

In the decree on the sacrificial aspect of the Mass, it is the third canon that stands out particularly.

> If anyone says that the sacrifice of the mass is only one of praise and thanksgiving, or that it is a mere commemoration of the sacrifice enacted on the cross and not itself appeasing; or that it avails only the one who receives and should not be offered for the living and the dead, for their sins, penalties, satisfactions and other needs: let him be anathema. [58]

We might summarise this teaching, in turn, by saying that it expresses the Catholic conviction that, in the Mass, there is a *real engagement* with the one sacrifice of Christ on Calvary. What Trent means by 'appeasing' or 'propitiatory' can be deduced from the contrast it makes; what it is rejecting is the idea that the Mass is 'a mere commemoration' of Christ's sacrifice, as if that sacrifice happened long ago and all that we can do now is give God praise and thanksgiving for it. In accordance with the scriptures, as we saw in section 6, above, Catholic belief is that that sacrifice, which indeed took place once and for all long ago, is nevertheless engraved in the heavens and overarches history, such that it can be present, and indeed, *is* present in our midst in all its redeeming power in every Mass, so that we can enter into it more fully and reap its fruits for the living and the dead, together with the other benefits that Trent lists.

We may say that, in an understandable reaction against the mistaken suspicion that there was a *repetition* of the sacrifice of Christ taking place in the Mass, the Reformers swung to the other extreme and denied any sacrificial aspect of the Mass. What Trent was reasserting was that there is no repetition of Christ's sacrifice in the Mass, but that the Mass is sacrificial because his once and for all sacrifice is truly present among us in all its power.

Before moving on from Trent, we should note its teaching that, after the consecration, our Lord Jesus Christ, true God and true man, is really and fully present under both forms of bread and wine,[59] so that he is fully received under either form. We should also note its teaching on the *forgiveness* that there is in the Eucharist. The *Catechism* reiterates Trent when it teaches that the Eucharist is 'a remedy to free us from our daily faults' (*CCC* 1394-5, 1436), and that the sacrament of reconciliation exists, above all, for those who, after Baptism, have fallen into grave sin (*CCC* 1446). This again leads us to think of the significance of receiving the blood of the Lord, particularly symbolised by receiving communion from the cup. The wine is consecrated and becomes the blood of Christ 'shed for you and for all so that sins may be forgiven', so receiving the blood of the Lord in the Eucharist is surely an excellent way to express sorrow for our sins and the desire to wash the baptismal robes that we have stained by our sins white again in the blood of the Lamb (cf *Rev* 7:14). Sorrow for our sins and the desire for forgiveness are vital aspects of the renewing of our discipleship that we express as we take the cup and drink, as we saw above (section 8c). As we have repeatedly seen (cf also section 4, above), there are great benefits for our Christian lives and for our catechesis in receiving communion under both kinds!

d. Second Vatican Council (1962 - 1965)

The teaching of the Council of Trent is decisive for Catholic understanding of the Eucharist, but we need to see how what it said in those two decrees, eleven years apart, can be held together, so as to nip in the bud any danger of misunderstanding the Eucharist.

We saw earlier, in section 6, that the scriptures teach that, in the Eucharist, we have an encounter with the heavenly liturgy. This, too, happens by the power of the Holy Spirit (cf section 1), about whom Jesus significantly said at the Last Supper: 'when the Spirit of truth comes he will lead you to the complete truth, ... and he will reveal to you the things to come' (*Jn* 16:13). At the centre of that heavenly assembly stands Christ, the victorious Lamb of God, as we saw. *That* is the Christ who is really present in the Mass, Christ as he is today, risen and glorious. But we also saw that the victorious Christ is holding, as it were, his precious blood, the 'purifying blood which pleads more insistently than Abel's' (*Heb* 12:24), and that the Lamb bore the marks of having been slain (*Rev* 5:6). Calvary has not been forgotten, and therefore as soon as Christ is present, so too is his sacrifice, which he bears in himself for evermore. Since he is present sacramentally, so too is his sacrifice. In other words, the Eucharist, properly understood, is a *sacramental sacrifice*. The most notable ecumenical statement of recent times, in which the Catholic Church was fully involved, signalled a most welcome agreement on this point when it simply said: 'The Eucharist is the sacrament of the unique sacrifice of Christ, who ever lives to make intercession for us'.[60]

In addition to the many points we have already noted from Vatican II, let us now finally see how the Council presented this very important integrated understanding of the Eucharist. In the Body of Christ, it taught, 'the life of Christ is communicated to those who believe and who, through the sacraments, are united in a hidden and real way to Christ in his passion and glorification'. As soon as we are united with Christ, we are united with his passion and glorification, because they are inseparable from him. This is most especially true of the Eucharist. 'Really sharing in the body of the Lord in the breaking of the eucharistic bread, we are taken up into communion with him and with one another' (*LG* 7).

Here is concentrated all that we have seen. Communion with God in Christ in the Eucharist brings us into communion with one another, the Eucharist makes the Church; and that communion with God in Christ is a communion in Christ's own sacrifice and self-gift to his Father. Of its very nature, that communion should move us to give ourselves more deeply to God in Christ, and also to one another, and to the world at large.

God so loved the world that he gave his only Son, that whoever believes in him should not perish but have eternal life (Jn 3:16; RSV).

In the Eucharist, we receive the body of Christ in order to become the Body of Christ, the body of the one who was sent into the world because the Father so loved the world. It immediately follows that we ourselves, having received, are sent out to proclaim the good news.

In fact, in the celebration of the Eucharist, the dynamism of Pentecost day is renewed. On that day, the Holy Spirit descended on the apostles and they immediately went out to proclaim the Gospel (*Acts* 2:1-41). In every Eucharist, likewise, the Spirit descends not only upon the gifts of bread and wine to transform them into the body and blood of the Lord, but also upon the community that receives: 'Grant that we, who are nourished by his body and blood, may be filled with his Holy Spirit, and become one body, one spirit in Christ' (Eucharistic Prayer III). Having received communion, the community is then sent out: 'Go in peace to love and serve the Lord'. De Lubac made the thoughtful observation that: 'Our churches are the "upper room" where not only is the Last Supper renewed but Pentecost also'.[61]

Given that being grafted into the mystery of Pentecost is often how we describe the effect of the sacrament of Confirmation, we see that, as well as renewing the washing of Baptism, every Eucharist also renews the anointing of Confirmation, and there is, therefore, logic and coherence in the order in which the Church always speaks of these three sacraments of initiation, namely:

Baptism, Confirmation, Eucharist (e.g. *LG* 11; *CCC* 1212). In that light, it seems odd to celebrate Eucharist, in which the grace of Pentecost is renewed, without having been grafted into that mystery by Confirmation! We can therefore understand why various dioceses around the world have now changed their policy so as to celebrate Confirmation before First Holy Communion for children, in other words, according to the same sequence that is followed whenever an adult is initiated: Baptism, then Confirmation, then Eucharist.

10. CONCLUSION

After his Resurrection, Jesus appeared to two of his disciples on the road to Emmaus. The account of their meeting (*Lk* 24:13-35) essentially traces the very form of the celebration of the Eucharist, as Jesus first unfolds the scriptures to them and then breaks bread with them. Having initially been downcast, they went from their encounter full of joy, their hearts burning within them, to share the good news of 'what had happened on the road and how they had recognised him in the breaking of bread' (*Lk* 24:35). Having been unsure of his Resurrection, now they knew that it was true. Like them, the Church all through the ages has gone on encountering the Risen Christ in the breaking of bread with wonder and joy. Like them, we too are called to go out from the Eucharist to proclaim the victory of hope over fear, the victory of communion over separation, and the victory of life over death.

FURTHER READING

Many of the topics dealt with in this booklet are more fully treated in my book, *Sacrament of Salvation,* see details below.

1. Official texts (showing the abbreviations used in the text)

Pope Paul VI, Encyclical Letter, *Mysterium Fidei* (1965)

Pope John Paul II, Apostolic Letter, *Dies Domini* (1998) - Encyclical Letter, *Ecclesia de Eucharistia* ('EDE', 2003)

Second Vatican Council, Constitution on the Sacred Liturgy, *Sacrosanctum Concilium* ('*SC*', 1963) - Dogmatic Constitution on the Church, *Lumen Gentium* ('*LG*', 1964) - Pastoral Constitution on the Church in the Modern World, *Gaudium et Spes* ('*GS*', 1965)

Catechism of the Catholic Church ('*CCC*'; London: Geoffrey Chapman, 1994), particularly §§1322-1419 on 'The Sacrament of the Eucharist'

Catholic Bishops' Conferences of England & Wales, Ireland, and Scotland, *One Bread One Body* (London/Dublin: CTS/Veritas, 1998)

2. Ecumenical texts

Anglican-Roman Catholic International Commission (ARCIC), Statement on 'Eucharistic Doctrine' (1971), and Elucidation (1979), in *The Final Report* (London: CTS/SPCK, 1982).

Joint International Commission for Theological Dialogue between the Roman Catholic Church and the Orthodox Church, Agreed Statement, 'The Mystery of the Church and of the Eucharist in the Light of the Mystery of the Holy Trinity'

(1982), cf Paul McPartlan (ed.), *One in 2000? Towards Catholic-Orthodox Unity* (Slough: St Paul, 1993), pp.37-52.

World Council of Churches, Faith and Order Commission, *Baptism, Eucharist and Ministry* (The 'Lima Report'; Faith and Order Paper 111: Geneva, 1982).

3. Useful books

Bouyer, Louis, *Eucharist. Theology and Spirituality of the Eucharistic Prayer* (Indiana: Univ. of Notre Dame, 1968)

Crockett, William R., *Eucharist: Symbol of Transformation* (New York: Pueblo, 1989)

Dix, Gregory, *The Shape of the Liturgy* (London: A & C Black, 1945)

Emminghaus, Johannes, *The Eucharist. Essence, Form, Celebration* (Collegeville: Liturgical Press, 1997)

Gaudoin-Parker, Michael L., *The Real Presence through the ages* (New York: Alba House, 1993)

Jeremias, Joachim, *The Eucharistic Words of Jesus* (London: SCM, 1966)

Kodell, Jerome, *The Eucharist in the New Testament* (Collegeville: Liturgical Press, 1988)

LaVerdiere, Eugene, *The Eucharist in the New Testament and the Early Church* (New York: Pueblo, 1996)

Louth, Andrew (ed.), *Early Christian Writings* (Harmondsworth: Penguin, 1987)

de Lubac, Henri, *Catholicism* (San Francisco: Ignatius, 1988), particularly chap.3, 'The Sacraments'. - *The Splendour of the Church* (San Francisco: Ignatius, 1986), particularly chap.4, 'The Heart of the Church'.

McPartlan, Paul, *The Eucharist Makes the Church. Henri de Lubac and John Zizioulas in Dialogue* (Edinburgh: T & T Clark, 1993)* - *Sacrament of Salvation. An Introduction to Eucharistic Ecclesiology* (Edinburgh: T & T Clark, 1995; reprinted 2003)*

(* T & T Clark is now an imprint of Continuum, London)

Martos, Joseph, *Doors to the Sacred. A Historical Introduction to Sacraments in the Catholic Church* (Liguori, Missouri: Triumph Books, 1991), particularly chapter eight, 'Eucharist'.

Moloney, Raymond, *The Eucharist* (London: Geoffrey Chapman, 1995)

Nichols, Aidan, *The Holy Eucharist* (Dublin: Veritas, 1991)

Rordorf, Willy, and others, *The Eucharist of the Early Christians* (New York: Pueblo, 1978)

Yarnold, Edward, *The Awe-Inspiring Rites of Initiation* (Edinburgh: T & T Clark, 1994)

Zizioulas, John, *Being as Communion* (London: Darton, Longman & Todd, 1985), particularly chapter four, 'Eucharist and Catholicity'.

The abbreviation *'PL'* used when citing some of the Church Fathers refers to: J. P .Migne, *Patrologia Latina* (Paris, 1844-64).

The abbreviation *'DS'* used when citing various Church documents refers to: Denzinger-Schönmetzer, *Enchiridion Symbolorum Definitionum et Declarationum* (Freiburg: Herder, 1976).

On the Sacraments:

Baptism (CTS Publications, 2004; Do 712).
Confirmation (CTS Publications, 2004; Do 713).
Eucharist (CTS Publications, 2004; Do 714).
Reconciliation (CTS Publications, 2004; Do 716).
Anointing (CTS Publications, 2004; Do 711).
Marriage (CTS Publications, 2004; Do 710).
Holy Orders (CTS Publications, 2004; Do 715).

ENDNOTES

[1] Biblical references are taken from the *New Jerusalem Bible* (London: Darton, Longman & Todd, 1985), unless otherwise indicated.

[2] All Vatican II documents are quoted from A.Flannery, *Vatican Council II. The Conciliar and PostConciliar Documents* (Dublin: Dominican Publications, 1981).

[3] Henri de Lubac, *The Splendour of the Church* (San Francisco: Ignatius, 1986), pp.134, 152; cf Paul McPartlan, *The Eucharist Makes the Church. Henri de Lubac and John Zizioulas in Dialogue* (Edinburgh: T & T Clark, 1993), p.xv, and passim.

[4] Joseph Ratzinger, *Principles of Catholic Theology* (San Francisco: Ignatius, 1987), p.53.

[5] Agreed Statement, 'The Mystery of the Church and of the Eucharist in the Light of the Mystery of the Holy Trinity' (1982), I,5,c; cf Paul McPartlan (ed.), *One in 2000? Towards Catholic-Orthodox Unity* (Slough: St Paul, 1993), pp.40-41.

[6] Cf Pope John Paul II, Apostolic Letter, *Dies Domini* (1998).

[7] Jurgen Moltmann, *The Church in the Power of the Spirit* (London: SCM, 1992), p.256.

[8] Pope John Paul II, Encyclical Letter, *Ecclesia de Eucharistia* (2003; hereafter, EDE), 15.

[9] EDE, 11.

[10] EDE, 3.

[11] EDE, 15.

[12] There is a good treatment of the accounts in Jerome Kodell, *The Eucharist in the New Testament* (Collegeville: Liturgical Press, 1988), and a helpful tabulation of them on pp.58-59.

[13] EDE, 5.

[14] For an exploration of the links between the Eucharist and the Church, see Paul McPartlan, *Sacrament of Salvation. An Introduction to Eucharistic Ecclesiology* (Edinburgh: T & T Clark, 1995; reprinted 2003).

[15] Cf Catholic Bishops' Conferences of England & Wales, Ireland, and Scotland, *One Bread One Body* (London/Dublin: CTS/Veritas, 1998).

[16] *General Instruction of the Roman Missal* (1970), n.240; cf 2002 edition, n.281. See further below, sections 8c and 9c.

[17] See below, section 9c, on the Council of Trent.

[18] John A. T. Robinson, *The Body. A Study in Pauline Theology* (London: SCM, 1952), p.28.

[19] Joseph A. Fitzmeyer, 'Pauline Theology', in R.Brown, J.Fitzmeyer, R.E.Murphy, (eds.), *The Jerome Biblical Commentary* (London: Geoffrey Chapman, 1969), p.815, § 79:87.

[20] Cf Anglican-Roman Catholic International Commission (ARCIC), Statement on 'Eucharistic Doctrine' (1971), 5; in *The Final Report* (London: CTS/SPCK, 1982), p.14.

[21] Pope St Leo the Great, *Serm.* 63,7 (PL 54, 357C), quoted in *Lumen Gentium* 26. Leo was pope from 440 to 461.

[22] De Lubac, *The Splendour of the Church* (San Francisco: Ignatius, 1986), p.203.

[23] *Lumen Gentium* 1 (quoted above, in section 3), cf LG 9, 48; also in the Pastoral Constitution on the Church in the Modern World, *Gaudium et Spes,* 42, 45.

[24] See above, section 3.

[25] Henri de Lubac, *Corpus Mysticum* (1949), p.283; cf Paul McPartlan, *The Eucharist Makes the Church,* p.80.

[26] *Roman Missal,* Preface of Sundays in Ordinary Time 1.

[27] For a survey of the patristic, scholastic and modern periods, see my book, *Sacrament of Salvation,* chapter three.

[28] For an account of recent, very fruitful ecumenical dialogue on the Eucharist, see *Sacrament of Salvation,* chapter six.

[29] Ignatius, *Smyrnaeans* 8, in Andrew Louth (ed.), *Early Christian Writings* (Harmondsworth: Penguin, 1987), p.103.

[30] Ignatius, Ephesians 20, in *Early Christian Writings,* p.66.

[31] Smyrnaeans 4; *Early Christian Writings,* p.102.

[32] Smyrnaeans 1 & 3; *Early Christian Writings,* p.101.

[33] Smyrnaeans 1; *Early Christian Writings,* p.101.

[34] Smyrnaeans 7; *Early Christian Writings,* p.102.

[35] Cf Paul F. Bradshaw, *The Search for the Origins of Christian Worship* (London: SPCK, 2002), particularly chapter four.

[36] *Apostolic Tradition* 3,4; cf Paul F. Bradshaw, Maxwell E. Johnson, L. Edward Phillips, *The Apostolic Tradition* (Minneapolis: Fortress, 2002), p.30.

[37] Cyprian, *Letter* 63,17,1; in G.W.Clarke (ed.), *The Letters of Cyprian of Carthage* (Ancient Christian Writers, vol.46; New York: Newman, 1986), p.107.

[38] Cyprian, *Letter* 57,3,2; in Clarke (ed.), Letters, p.57.

[39] Quoting Cyprian, *De oratione dominica* 23 (PL 4, 556).

[40] Cyprian, *Letter* 63,13,4; in *Letters,* p.105.

[41] Cyprian, *Letter* 57,2,2; in *Letters,* p.56.

[42] Cyprian, *Letter* 57,3,2; in *Letters,* p.57.

[43] Cf my book, *Sacrament of Salvation,* chapter seven.

[44] Ambrose, *De Sacramentis*, 4,14-15; quoted from Edward Yarnold, *The Awe-Inspiring Rites of Initiation* (Edinburgh: T & T Clark, 1994), pp.132-133. This book valuably contains four sets of baptismal homilies from leading bishops of the fourth century.

[45] Augustine, *Tractates on the Gospel of John* 26,13; quoted in *CCC* 1398. Cf Henri de Lubac, *Catholicism* (San Francisco: Ignatius, 1988), p.98.

[46] Saint Augustine, *Confessions* (ed. Henry Chadwick; Oxford, 1991) 7,10,16 (p.124).

[47] Augustine, *Sermon* 272; quoted by de Lubac, *Catholicism*, p.92.

[48] Augustine, *Tractates on the Gospel of John* 26,17; trans. by John W. Rettrig, in *The Fathers of the Church,* vol.79 (Washington: Catholic University of America, 1988), p.274.

[49] Augustine, *Contra Faustum* 12,20.

[50] De Lubac, *Corpus Mysticum,* p.269.

[51] Cf Pope Paul VI, Encyclical Letter, *Mysterium Fidei* (1965), which reasserted the doctrine of 'transubstantiation', and judged 'trans-signification' and 'trans-finalisation' to be inadequate explanations (n.12).

[52] For a fuller account of the shift from a communion model to a pyramid model, see my book, *Sacrament of Salvation,* chapter three.

[53] Joseph Ratzinger, *Principles of Catholic Theology* (San Francisco: Ignatius, 1987), pp.254-255.

[54] T. Cranmer, *Writings and Disputations Relative to the Sacrament of the Lord's Supper* (1844), p.6; quoted by Raymond Moloney, *The Eucharist* (London: Geoffrey Chapman, 1995), p.154.

[55] There is a valuable discussion of the decrees and of the overall teaching of the Council in its historical context in R.Moloney, *The Eucharist,* chapter ten.

[56] The canons of the two decrees are cited from Norman P. Tanner (ed.), *Decrees of the Ecumenical Councils* (London: Sheed & Ward, 1990), vol.2, pp.*697-698; and *735-736, respectively.

[57] Cf Carl E. Braaten, Robert W. Jenson (eds.), *Union with Christ. The New Finnish Interpretation of Luther* (Grand Rapids: Eerdmans, 1998).

[58] See above, note 56.

[59] *Decree on the Most Holy Sacrament of the Eucharist,* chapter one; cf Tanner (ed.), *Decrees of the Ecumenical Councils,* vol.2, p.*693.

[60] World Council of Churches, Faith and Order Commission, *Baptism, Eucharist and Ministry* (The 'Lima Report'; Faith and Order Paper 111: Geneva, 1982), 'Eucharist', 8; cf EDE 12.

[61] De Lubac, *Catholicism,* p.111.